THE FABULOUS LOST & FOUND

AND THE LITTLE MOUSE WHO SPOKE CROATIAN

WRITTEN BY MARK PALLIS
ILLUSTRATED BY PETER BAYNTON

NEU WESTEND
— PRESS —

For Lucy and Emily - MP

For Hannah and Skye - PB

THE FABULOUS LOST & FOUND AND THE LITTLE MOUSE WHO SPOKE CROATIAN

First Printing, 2021
ISBN: 978-1-913595-76-0
NeuWestendPress.com

THE FABULOUS LOST & FOUND

AND THE LITTLE MOUSE WHO SPOKE CROATIAN

WRITTEN BY MARK PALLIS
ILLUSTRATED BY PETER BAYNTON

NEU WESTEND
— PRESS —

In the middle of the big city is a tiny yellow building. If anyone loses anything, this is where it ends up.

It is called the Lost and Found.

Mr and Mrs Frog keep everything safe, hoping that someday every lost watch and bag and phone and toy and shoe and cheesegrater will find its owner again.

But the shop is very small and there are so many lost things. It is all quite a squeeze, but still, it's fabulous.

One sunny day, a little mouse walked in.

“Welcome,” said Mrs Frog. “What have you lost?”

“Izgubio sam šešir,” said the mouse.

Mr and Mrs Frog could not speak Croatian. They had no idea what the little mouse was saying.

What shall we do? they wondered.

Maybe she's lost an umbrella. Everyone loses an umbrella at least twice, thought Mr Frog.

"Have you lost this?" asked Mr Frog.

“Kišobran? Ne,” replied the mouse.

Then Mrs Frog remembered something that had been handed in a few months ago...

“Is this yours?” Mrs Frog asked, holding up a chunk of cheese.

“Sir? Ne. Smrdi!” said the mouse.

“Time to put that cheese in the bin dear,” said Mr Frog.

"Maybe the word 'Šešir' means coat," said Mr Frog.

"Now where did I put that nice yellow one?"

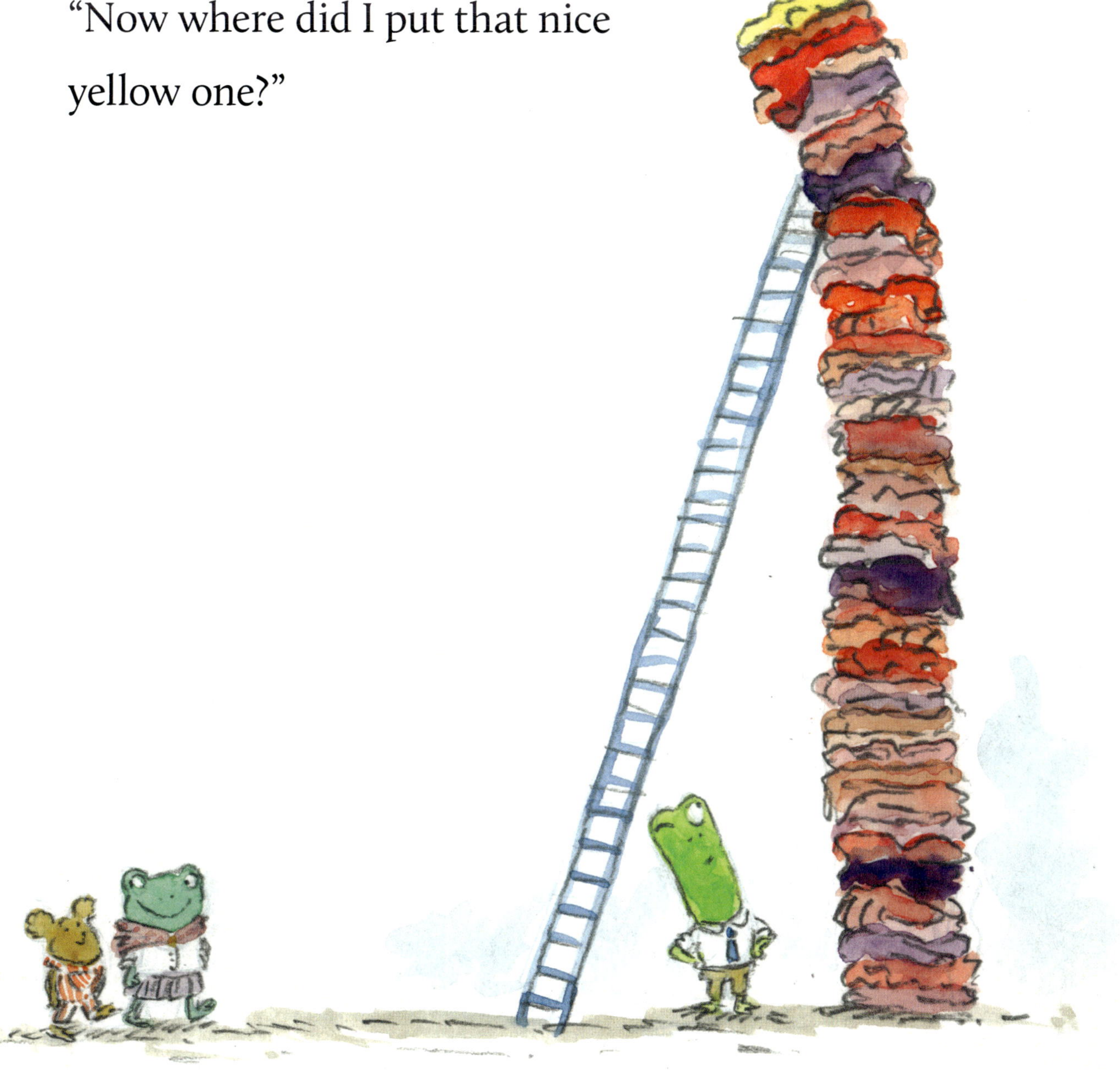

"Got it!" said Mr Frog.

“Kaput? Ne. Izgubio sam šešir,”
said the mouse.

She was starting to feel a bit frustrated.

“We need to keep trying,” said Mrs Frog.

Ni šal.

Ne hlače.

Ni džemper.

Ne sunčane naočale.

Ne cipele.

“Izgubio sam šešir,” said the mouse.

Ni dva bicikla.
Ni računalo.

Ne tri knjige.

Ne četiri banane.

Ni pet tipki.

It was no good. A fat wet tear rolled down the mouse's cheek.

“How about a nice cup of tea?” asked Mrs Frog kindly.

“Obožavam čaj. Hvala,” replied the mouse. They sat together, sipping their tea and all feeling a bit sad.

Suddenly, the mouse realised she could try pointing.

She pointed at her head.

"Šešir!" she said.

"I've got it!" exclaimed Mrs Frog, leaping up.

“A wig of course!” said Mrs Frog.

“Ni perika,” said the mouse.

Nije crvena.

Nije plavuša.

Nije smeđa.

Ne zeleno.

Ne raznobojan.

"What about this?" asked Mr Frog, pulling back a curtain.

"Šešir!," exclaimed the mouse.

"Ah, so 'Šešir' means hat. Wonderful!" Mr and Mrs Frog cheered.

Previsok.

Premalen.

Preuzak.

Prevelik.

"One hat left," said Mrs Frog, reaching all the way to the back of the cupboard.

"It couldn't be this old thing, could it?"

“Moja kapa.

Pronašao sam svoj šešir!

Hvala vam puno,” said the mouse.

And just like that, the mouse found her hat.

"Doviđenja," she said, as she skipped away.
"Doviđenja," replied Mr and Mrs Frog.

"I wonder who will come tomorrow?" said Mr Frog.
Mrs Frog put her arm around him.

"I don't know," she replied, giving him a squeeze,
"but whoever it is, we'll do our best to help."

LEARNING TO LOVE LANGUAGES

An additional language opens a child's mind, broadens their horizons and enriches their emotional life. Research has shown that the time between a child's birth and their sixth or seventh birthday is a "golden period" when they are most receptive to new languages. This is because they have an in-built ability to distinguish the sounds they hear and make sense of them. The Story-powered Language Learning Method taps into these natural abilities.

HOW THE STORY-POWERED LANGUAGE LEARNING METHOD WORKS

We create an emotionally engaging and funny story for children and adults to enjoy together, just like any other picture book. Studies show that social interaction, like enjoying a book together, is critical in language learning.

Through the story, we introduce a relatable character who speaks only in the new language. This helps build empathy and a positive attitude towards people who speak different languages. These are both important aspects in laying the foundations for lasting language acquisition in a child's life.

As the story progresses, the child naturally works with the characters to discover the meaning of a wide range of fun new words. Strategic use of humour ensures that this subconscious learning is rewarded with laughter; the child feels good and the first seeds of a lifelong love of languages are sown.

For more information and free downloads visit www.neuwestendpress.com

ALL THE BEAUTIFUL CROATIAN WORDS AND PHRASES FROM OUR STORY

Izgubio sam šešir	*I've lost my hat*
kišobran	*umbrella*
sir	*cheese*
smrdi	*it stinks*
kaput	*coat*
šal	*scarf*
hlače	*trousers*
sunčane naočale	*sunglasses*
džemper	*sweater*
cipele	*shoes*
jedan	*one*
Dva	*two*
Tri	*three*
Četiri	*four*
Pet	*five*
Računalo	*computer*
knjiga	*book*
Ključ	*key*
banana	*banana*
bicikl	*bicycle*
Volim čaj	*I love tea*
Hvala vam	*thank you*
Hvala vam puno	*thank you very much*
perika	*wig*
crvena	*red*
plavokosa	*blond*
smeđa	*brown*
zeleno	*green*
raznobojne	*multicoloured*
ne	*no*
moja kapa	*my hat*
previsok	*too tall*
prevelik	*too big*
premalen	*too small*
preuzak	*too tight*
Pronašao sam svoj šešir	*I've found my hat*
Doviđenja	*goodbye*

You can learn more words and phrases with these hilarious, heartwarming stories from NEU WESTEND — PRESS —

Available in over 50 different languages!

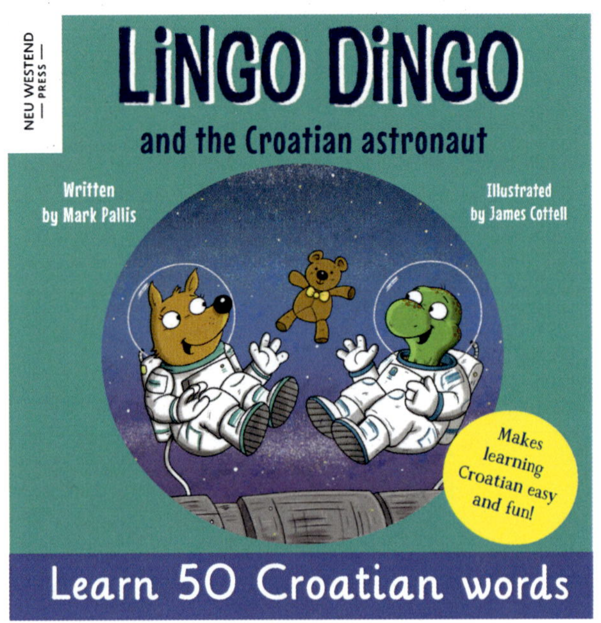

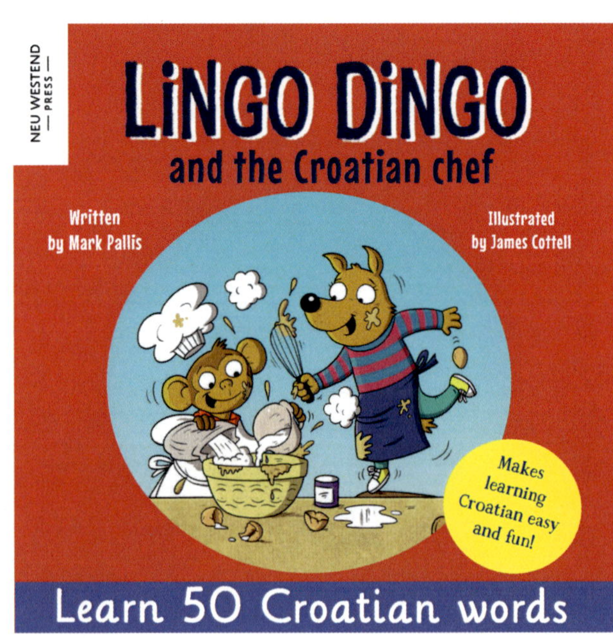

Go for it!

@MARK_PALLIS on twitter
www.markpallis.com

To download your FREE certifcate, and more cool stuff, visit www.markpallis.com

“I want people to be so busy laughing, they don’t realise they’re learning!”

Mark Pallis

Crab and Whale is the bestselling story of how a little Crab helps a big Whale. It’s carefully designed to help even the most energetic children find a moment of calm and focus. It also includes a special mindful breathing exercise and affirmation for children. Also available in French, Spanish and German.

Featured as one of Mindful.org’s ‘Seven Mindful Children’s books’

Do you call them hugs or cuddles?

In this funny, heartwarming story, you will laugh out loud as two loveable gibbons try to figure out if a hug is better than a cuddle and, in the process, learn how to get along.

A perfect story for anyone who loves a hug (or a cuddle!)

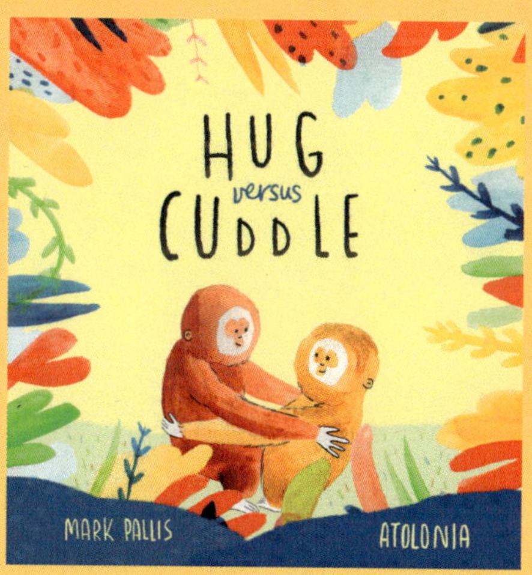

www.markpallis.com

Made in the USA
Middletown, DE
13 January 2026